Annie Oakley

History Maker Bios

Ginger Wadsworth

LERNER PUBLICATIONS COMPANY • MINNEAPOLIS

To Carolyn Mills, Annie Oakley wannabe

*The details of Annie Oakley's life vary across sources. The key
sources used for this book are Glenda Riley's* The Life and Legacy
of Annie Oakley *and Shirl Kasper's* Annie Oakley.

Illustrations by Tim Parlin

Text copyright © 2005 by Ginger Wadsworth
Illustrations copyright © 2005 by Lerner Publications Company

Lerner Publications Company
A division of Lerner Publishing Group
241 First Avenue North
Minneapolis, MN 55401 U.S.A.

Website address: www.lernerbooks.com

Library of Congress Cataloging-in-Publication Data

Wadsworth, Ginger.
    Annie Oakley / by Ginger Wadsworth.
       p.   cm. — (History maker bios)
    Includes bibliographical references and index.
    ISBN-13: 978–0–8225–2940–8 (lib. bdg. : alk. paper)
    ISBN-10: 0–8225–2940–8 (lib. bdg. : alk. paper)
      1. Oakley, Annie, 1860–1926—Juvenile literature. 2. Shooters of firearms—
United States—Biography—Juvenile literature. 3. Entertainer—Juvenile
literature. I. Parlin, Tim, ill. II. Title. III. Series.
    GV1157.O3W33 2005
    799.3'.092—dc22   2005000582

Manufactured in the United States of America
1 2 3 4 5 6 – JR – 10 09 08 07 06 05

Table of Contents

COPYRIGHT 1899
RICHARD K. FOX

Alameda Free Library

1550 Oak St.

Alameda, CA 94501

510-747-7777

Date: 3/9/2018

Time: 2:32:55 PM

Fines/Fees Owed: $0.00

Total Checked Out: 4

Checked Out

Title: The crochet answer book : solutions to
every problem you'll ever face, answers to every
question you'll ever ask
Barcode: 33341007826695
Due Date: 03/30/2018 23:59:59

Title: The chicks with sticks' guide to crochet :
learn to crochet with more than thirty cool, easy
patterns
Barcode: 33341007416968
Due Date: 03/30/2018 23:59:59

Title: Charlie and the chocolate factory
Barcode: 33341007789349
Due Date: 03/30/2018 23:59:59

Title: Crochet basics : all you need to know to
get hooked on crochet
Barcode: 33341007259921
Due Date: 03/30/2018 23:59:59

INTRODUCTION

Annie Oakley grew up in a poor but loving family on an Ohio farm. She learned about hunting from her father. When she was eight, she fired her first rifle to provide food for her starving family. In the late 1800s, Annie began shooting in front of audiences. She starred in many shows throughout the years, performing for a queen, princes, and ordinary people all over the world.

Annie is still considered the United States' greatest female sharpshooter. But she was more than a star. Annie taught classes about gun safety. She gave away her money to children who lived in orphanages.

This is her story.

1 A HARD LIFE

Phoebe Ann Moses was born on
August 13, 1860, in western Ohio.
Her family called her Annie. Annie lived in a
small cabin with her parents, sisters, and
brother. Her mother and father, Susan and
Jacob Moses, were farmers.

Cornfields surrounded the family's cabin. A big forest grew at the edge of the fields. The Moses family had to travel a whole day to reach a nearby town.

The United States was fighting the Civil War when Annie was young. The northern half of the country was battling the South. Annie's parents were Quakers. This religious group does not believe in war. Jacob Moses owned a gun only to hunt for food and to protect his family.

In the early nineteenth century, many families like Annie's lived in homes built of logs.

Growing up, Annie was a tomboy. She did not like playing inside with her sisters and their rag dolls. Instead, Annie helped her father do farmwork. She also went hunting with him. She learned about the forest animals and plants.

Jacob Moses died when Annie was five. Then her sister Mary Jane died. It was a sad time for the family. They had to move to a smaller, rented farm. The children fed the animals, washed clothes, and weeded the garden. They helped store food for the long, cold Ohio winters. No one went to school or played games.

When Annie was a child, many families used wood fires to cook and to heat their homes. Children helped gather wood to keep these fires burning.

Mrs. Moses didn't have enough food for her children. She had to send them away for a while. Annie's brother and sister moved to a nearby farm. Annie stayed with family friends who ran a home for the poor. It was called the Darke County Infirmary. Annie got a bed to sleep in and plenty of food there. She also learned how to knit and mend clothes.

Darke County Infirmary

THE WOLVES

When Annie was about ten, a family hired her to work as a mother's helper. She went to live with them on their farm. The family told Annie she could hunt and go to school. It sounded perfect! But the family lied. They made Annie begin her chores at four in the morning. If she didn't finish the work, they beat her. Annie called the family "the wolves" because they were so cruel. Finally, she ran away from the farm. She went back to live at the home for the poor.

Annie worked hard at the home for the poor. She began to learn how to read and write. But she missed her family. Annie moved back home when she was about fifteen. She began hunting for food with her father's gun. She almost never missed her target. Annie made sure her family had more than enough meat to eat.

Annie hunted nearly every day. She filled baskets with the quail and rabbits that her family did not need. A local store owner bought the extra game. Some of it ended up in hotel restaurants in big cities, such as Cincinnati. Annie earned a lot of money for her work as a hunter. She surprised her mother by paying her bills for her.

Annie's hunting skill fed her family and helped pay their bills.

In 1875, Annie visited Cincinnati. She stayed with one of her married sisters. It was Annie's first time in a city. Annie had never seen so many buildings, animals, or people in one place. Steamboats moved up and down the Ohio River, and pioneers rolled west in covered wagons.

Some of the men in town belonged to gun clubs. They practiced target shooting and competed with one another. Women could not join. But they could go to shooting galleries.

Cincinnati, Ohio, in the 1870s

Few women went to shooting galleries when Annie was young.

The shooting galleries were noisy places with many blinking lights. They had moving metal targets shaped like rabbits or bull's eyes. Annie ignored the confusion and picked up her gun. She easily hit all the targets!

News of Annie's skills spread quickly. In Cincinnati, she was invited to be in a shooting match. But to win the match, she would have to beat a man.

2 FAME

Annie competed against a well-known sharpshooter named Frank Butler. Frank shot first. He hit the target dead center. Then it was Annie's turn. Her knees were shaking, but she still hit the target. Frank and Annie kept shooting. Frank finally missed on the twenty-fifth shot. Annie didn't miss. She won a fifty-dollar prize. Even better, she won Frank's heart.

Frank and Annie

Frank Butler (BELOW RIGHT) and Annie started dating soon after they met. Frank's French poodle, George, delivered notes between the couple. Once the dog even brought Annie a box of candy!

Annie's mother didn't like Frank at first. He wasn't a Quaker, he was divorced with children, and he was ten years older than Annie. But then, Mrs. Moses saw how lovingly Frank treated her daughter. Soon she began to respect him.

Before long, Frank and Annie got married. Frank was the star in the family. He and his shooting partner, John Graham, traveled from town to town to perform in shows. These shows often had singers, animal acts, dancers, musicians, comedians, and acrobats too.

One day in 1882, John became sick just before going on stage. Annie stepped in to help. She wore a dress with a white collar, and her thick hair hung loose. The pretty little lady with the big gun fascinated the crowd. Annie and Frank took turns shooting, and Annie never missed. Everyone cheered! They didn't know that a woman could shoot so well.

Annie's shooting talent took people by surprise. Her style of dress was traditional, but her skill with guns was not.

That day, Annie became Frank's new partner. She chose her own stage name: Annie Oakley. The team of Oakley and Butler toured in the Midwest.

Annie designed and sewed all her own costumes. She always wore western-style clothes, a hat, and boots. She refused to wear pants because she did not think they were ladylike.

Annie always wore dresses at her shows.

Annie practiced hard between shows. She held her gun in her left hand, then in her right, and even upside down. She fired her gun again and again. Annie and Frank wanted to be the best shooting team in the country.

Soon Annie could shoot a playing card in half and snuff out a burning candle with a shot from her gun. Annie was a natural athlete. She jumped over a table, tossed some glass balls in the air, and then grabbed her rifle. She shot the glass balls in midair.

Annie practices shooting glass balls flung into the air. A Native American in the show watches her.

Sometimes Annie missed. She pretended to be sad and stomped her boots in the dust. But the crowds cheered even louder. She was the star of the show.

Annie and Frank joined the Sells Brothers Circus in 1884. They visited nearly two hundred cities that year. At night, Frank helped Annie with her reading and writing. She wrote letters to her family and sent them gifts and money. Annie was proud of the money she made. She said that "after the age of ten, I never had a nickel in my pocket that I didn't earn."

3 LITTLE SURE SHOT

After one of Annie's performances, Sitting Bull, a Lakota leader, asked to meet the star of the show. He told Annie that she reminded him of his daughter who had died.

Sitting Bull said he wanted to adopt Annie. He called her Watanya Cecila, which means "Little Sure Shot." Sitting Bull even gave Annie a pair of his daughter's moccasins. Sitting Bull and Annie became close friends.

Annie met Sitting Bull at her shooting exhibition in Saint Paul, Minnesota, in March 1884.

Frank wrote about Annie's friendship with Sitting Bull in a newspaper ad. He wanted people to know about Little Sure Shot. Annie had never been farther west than Kansas, but the ad made people think she came from the Wild West.

In 1885, Annie and Frank joined a show called Buffalo Bill's Wild West show. Performers in the show acted out a buffalo hunt and a stagecoach robbery. There were also shooting contests and cowboys twirling ropes. Smoking guns and the thunder of horses' hooves added to the excitement.

Performers act out a buffalo hunt in Buffalo Bill's Wild West show. Their guns made noise but did not use bullets.

WILD WEST SHOW

Buffalo Bill's Wild West show needed fifty train cars to carry its animals, people, and equipment. The train traveled at night to the next show grounds. Each morning, animal keepers led elk, buffalo, horses, and oxen off the train to graze beside the tracks. Buffalo Bill's show was like a small town. There was a repair shop, barbershop, wardrobe tent, and laundry. It took a long time to put the show together. Even the glass balls that Annie shattered during her performances were made on-site.

The leader of Buffalo Bill's Wild West called himself Buffalo Bill Cody. He had black eyes, long hair, and wore a large hat. He galloped in on his big gray horse to start each show. Then a band played the "Star-Spangled Banner." For the next three hours, families enjoyed the greatest outdoor show in American history.

When it was her turn, Annie always skipped in. She bowed, waved, and blew kisses. Annie was an actress as well as a sharpshooter. She loved to charm her audiences with her shooting skills. Her most famous trick started with a handheld mirror. Annie found her target in the mirror, aimed her gun back over her shoulder, and shot it without turning around. Afterward, she did a little jump-kick, then ran out of the arena.

Annie poses for a photograph to show how she uses her gun and mirror in her most famous shooting trick.

In later years, Annie added horseback-riding tricks to her act. She would ride at full speed in front of the crowd and then untie a handkerchief from her horse's hoof. After a lot of practice, she learned to stand on her horse's back while it galloped around the ring. These tricks made even more fans think of Annie as a western cowgirl.

Show posters featured many of the stunts that Annie's audiences liked the best.

Over time, Frank put away his guns and his high-top boots. He spent his time managing Annie's career. But nothing changed between Annie and Frank. Frank sometimes wrote poetry to Annie. He called her "his charming little girl" with "rain drops in her eyes."

Annie started the 1886 season with a long stay on Staten Island in New York. Everyone loved Buffalo Bill's Wild West *and* Little Sure Shot. Buffalo Bill decided to

move his show indoors to Madison Square Garden in the center of New York City. Crowds waited hours to get a look at Annie.

William F. Cody used the name "Buffalo Bill" for his Wild West show.

The next year, the Wild West show sailed for Great Britain. The show came to help Queen Victoria celebrate her fiftieth year as Great Britain's queen. For six months, the Wild West performers lived in tents near the city of London.

Annie got Sir Ralph, a Saint Bernard puppy, for a birthday gift in 1887. They posed for this photograph in a British photography studio.

Annie Oakley was very popular in Great Britain. Forty thousand to fifty thousand people came to her shows each day. Some of the people were royalty from Great Britain and other countries in Europe. Annie appeared after the ringmaster yelled, "Ladies and gentlemen, Miss Annie Oakley, the little girl of the Western Plains!"

4 STAGE STAR

The British read about Little Sure Shot in newspapers and in a popular booklet called *Rifle Queen*, which sold for two pennies. The author wrote that Annie battled wolves and grizzly bears, outrode a blizzard, and defeated a bad guy.

British fans liked the made-up stories about Annie's life on the U.S. frontier. Annie continued to dress for that role.

Annie tried to explain that the stories about her were made-up, but no one listened. Fans wanted to link Annie to cowboys, wild horses, and rugged frontier life in the United States. In Europe, Annie was becoming a superhero.

Buffalo Bill's Wild West show toured Europe again in 1889. This time, Annie performed in France, Italy, and Spain. The show returned to the United States in 1892. The performers went on the road, playing in hundreds of towns. Wherever Annie performed, she gave free tickets to children, especially orphans. She let the children sit in front and made sure they had plenty of popcorn, ice cream, and cold drinks.

In this photograph taken in 1890 in Rome, Italy, Buffalo Bill Cody appears on the left (CIRCLED) and Annie on the right (CIRCLED).

WEAPONS

In her Wild West shows, Annie used 12-gauge, double-barreled shotguns. The shotguns weighed about six pounds. Shotguns shoot pellets, which don't sail very far. That was important since so many people came to Annie's shows. Annie didn't want anyone to get hurt.

Thousands of people watched Annie perform. She was one of the best-known women in the United States. Annie liked her job. But she said she hoped "for the day when my work with the rifle and gun will be over with, and when I can take to the field and stream."

Annie and her dog go hunting.

Annie and Frank lived in a tent while they were in a traveling show. Annie carefully kept the tent homelike.

When they traveled, Annie and Frank often lived in a tent. Annie put up curtains and set out family photographs. She spread satin pillows, buffalo horns, and other treasures around the tent. Animal skins carpeted the floor. Guns were everywhere. There were often bouquets of flowers sent by admiring fans. Guests stopped by for tea and cakes. The tent was comfortable, but Annie dreamed of a real house.

Annie and Frank built their first home in New Jersey in 1893. They planned to live there part of the year. The three-story house had a stable for horses in the backyard. Annie bought fine dishes. She hired a cook and cleaning lady too. One room was filled with stuffed animals and skins. Annie often invited friends and family to visit.

Annie wrote letters, took walks, rode her horse, and practiced her shooting. Neighbors saw her bicycling through the fields with her gun and shooting at tin cans.

Between shows, Annie worked hard to keep her shooting and riding skills sharp. She also practiced new tricks.

Annie and Frank still toured with Buffalo Bill's Wild West show. But Annie was hurt in a serious train accident in 1901. The accident scared Annie, but it did not stop her career. She decided to try acting on stage. In 1902, Annie starred in *The Western Girl,* a show about a Colorado pioneer. Swinging a lasso, Annie captured the bad guy and saved the handsome hero from disaster. Audiences loved it.

5 LEAVING A LEGACY

L ife was changing for Annie and
Frank. Train travel was still popular,
but in 1903, Orville and Wilbur Wright flew
a controlled, powered airplane. Six years
later, Henry Ford introduced his Model T
car to the world. By 1910, the year Annie
turned fifty, millions of Americans traveled
by car.

Annie's hair turned white, and she wore glasses. Yet she was busier than ever. She still put on shows, and she began giving shooting lessons to women. "I would like . . . every woman to know how to handle firearms as naturally as they know how to handle babies," Annie explained. She wrote articles on the sport of shooting and a booklet on gun safety. She valued safety a great deal.

In 1909, Orville Wright thrilled a crowd in Fort Myer, Virginia, with a flight demonstration. Air shows gave Annie's shows tough competition.

Not too many people knew about another side to Annie. She still sent money and gifts to her family. Sometimes she gave money to orphanages. She may have helped as many as twenty young women with their school costs. Frank supported Annie's gift giving. Neither one complained about giving up something for themselves.

Annie (LEFT) and Frank (RIGHT) had a famous pet, Dave (CENTER). Dave went everywhere with them. Annie even signed her Christmas cards with Dave's name.

The United States entered World War I in 1917. Annie put on shooting shows at U.S. Army camps. She offered to train a women's division, in case the United States was attacked at home. But the secretary of war did not take Annie up on her offer.

DAVE WORKS FOR THE RED CROSS

During World War I, Annie and Frank held shows for the Red Cross, a group that helps people during war or disasters. Dave, their Irish setter, was part of the entertainment. Fans wrapped money in handkerchiefs and hid them. Then Annie blindfolded Dave. He trotted this way and that until he sniffed out the hidden money. Annie gave the money to the Red Cross.

World War I ended. So did the era of the fancy Wild West shows. People turned to a brand-new kind of entertainment—motion pictures. Some motion pictures, called westerns, were a little like Buffalo Bill's Wild West show. People liked to watch westerns on a big movie screen.

Annie's show business dreams ended in November of 1922 when she was in a car accident. Annie was badly hurt.

American inventor Thomas Alva Edison helped create motion pictures. He made a short film of Annie. His first movie projector was called the Edison Vitascope.

Annie recovered from her accident. She wore a leg brace, but she stayed cheerful and never complained. Annie started to write down her life story. Yet she didn't seem to have much energy. Annie could tell that she was dying.

Annie died on November 3, 1926, at the age of sixty-six. Frank was heartbroken. Eighteen days later, he died too.

Annie and Frank are buried side by side at Brock Cemetery in Darke County, Ohio.

Annie's fame grew after her death. Fans watched the 1935 movie *Annie Oakley* and attended a musical about Annie's life called *Annie Get Your Gun*. This musical still plays in theaters around the world.

The musical ANNIE GET YOUR GUN returned to Broadway in New York City for 1,045 shows between 1999 and 2001. Country music star Reba McEntire (LEFT) played Annie on Broadway for five months in 2001.

People who know Annie's story have written books about her. They have designed Annie Oakley-style clothes. Someone even created a television show about her.

Annie survived a hard childhood and became a role model to many women and girls. She showed that it was okay for women to ride, shoot, and hunt. She was one of the United States' first female sports stars, and she is still remembered as a strong heroine of the Wild West.

TIMELINE

ANNIE OAKLEY WAS BORN
IN WOODLAND, OHIO, ON
AUGUST 13, 1860.

In the year . . .

1866	Annie Oakley's father, Jacob Moses, died.	Age 5
1870	Annie moved to the Darke County Infirmary. she began working for the family she called "the wolves."	Age 10
1874	she became a hunter to earn money for her family.	
1875	she beat Frank Butler in a shooting match on Thanksgiving Day.	Age 15
1876	she married Frank on August 23.	
1882	she took the stage name Annie Oakley.	
1884	she toured with Sells Brothers Circus as Frank's shooting partner. she met Sitting Bull.	
1885	she joined Buffalo Bill's Wild West show.	Age 24
1887	she traveled to Great Britain with the show.	
1889	the Wild West show toured Europe.	
1901	she was injured in a train accident. she quit the Wild West show and tried acting on stage.	Age 41
1902	she starred in a stage play called *The Western Girl.*	
1915	she began teaching women to shoot.	
1917	the United States entered World War I.	
1918	Annie and Frank toured U.S. Army camps with their dog, Dave.	
1922	Annie was hurt in a car accident in Florida.	
1926	she died on November 3 in Ohio, near her birthplace. Frank died on November 21.	Age 66

ANNIE'S MOTTO

While working on her memoirs, Annie came up with a saying to explain how she felt about life. She printed this saying, or motto, on little cards. Annie's motto was "Aim at a high mark, and you'll hit it. No, not the first time, nor the second time, and maybe not the third. But keep on aiming and keep on shooting for only practice will make you perfect. Finally, you'll hit the bull's eye of success." Annie lived this motto every day. She always tried hard and never gave up.

All of her life, Annie worked hard. Her determination inspired many people.

FURTHER READING

Aller, Susan Bivin. *Sitting Bull.* Minneapolis: Lerner Publications Company, 2004. This biography tells all about Sitting Bull, the Lakota leader who befriended Annie Oakley.

Foran, Jill. *Annie Oakley.* New York: Weigl Publishers, 2003. This book provides information on folk hero Annie Oakley.

Krensky, Stephen. *Shooting for the Moon: The Amazing Life and Times of Annie Oakley.* New York: Melanie Kroupa Books, 2001. This picture-book biography examines the life of the famous sharpshooter.

Macy, Sue. *Bull's Eye: A Photobiography of Annie Oakley.* Washington, DC: National Geographic Society, 2001. This account of Annie Oakley's life includes photos and little-known facts about the star of the Wild West.

Ruffin, Frances E. *Annie Oakley.* New York: PowerKids Press, 2002. This book provides more details on the life of Annie Oakley.

WEBSITES

Annie Oakley (Buffalo Bill Historical Center)
http://www.bbhc.org/bbm/biographyAO.cfm
The website offers a brief biography and photographs of
Annie Oakley. It also includes links to information about
Buffalo Bill and his Wild West show.

National Women's Hall of Fame
http://www.greatwomen.org
Visit this site for information on Annie Oakley and other
great women from American history.

Ohio Biography: Annie Oakley
http://ohiobio.org/oakley.htm
Ohiobio.org has a biography of Annie Oakley. It also
includes information about other famous Ohioans.

SELECT BIBLIOGRAPHY

Alderman, Clifford Lindsey. *Annie Oakley and the World of
    Her Time.* New York: Macmillan Publishing Co., Inc.,
    1979.

Havighurst, Walter. *Annie Oakley of the Wild West.* New
    York: The Macmillan Company, 1954.

Kasper, Shirl. *Annie Oakley.* Norman: University of
    Oklahoma Press, 1992.

Riley, Glenda. *The Life and Legacy of Annie Oakley.*
    Norman: University of Oklahoma Press, 1994.

Sayers, Isabelle S. *Annie Oakley and Buffalo Bill's Wild
    West.* New York: Dover Publications, Inc., 1981.

INDEX

Acknowledgments

For photographs and artwork: The images in this book are used with the permission of: Library of Congress, pp. 4 (LC-USZ62-7873), 7(LC-USZ62-6951), 13 (LC-USZ62-134450), 21 (LC-USZ62-111147), 26 (LC-USZC4-3116), 37 (LC-USZ62-89971), 40 (LC-USZC4-1102); © North Wind Picture Archives, pp. 8, 22; Courtesy of Karen Allen, p. 9; Ohio Historical Society, pp. 11, 41; © Brown Brothers, p. 12; Garst Museum, Greenville, Ohio, pp. 15, 38; © Western History Collection, University of Oklahoma Library, p. 16; Denver Public Library, Western History Collection, pp. 17, 18, 30, 31, 33, 34, 45; Courtesy Buffalo Bill Historical Center, Cody, Wyoming, pp. 24, 27, 32; Circus World Museum, p. 25; © Spencer Platt/Newsmakers/Getty Images, p. 42. Front cover: Garst Museum, Greenville, Ohio. Back cover: Museum of the American West Collection, Autry National Center.

For quoted material: pp. 19, 26, Glenda Riley, *The Life and Legacy of Annie Oakley* (Norman: University of Oklahoma Press, 1994); p. 28, Jean Flynn, *Annie Oakley: Legendary Sharpshooter* (Springfield, NJ: Enslow Publishers, Inc., 1998); pp. 32, 45, Shirl Kasper, *Annie Oakley* (Norman: University of Oklahoma Press, 1992); p. 37, Sue Macy, *Bull's Eye: A Photobiography of Annie Oakley* (Washington, DC: National Geographic Society, 2001).